T0156769

Just Ask!

1000 QUESTIONS TO GROW YOUR RELATIONSHIP

Michele O'Mara, PhD

authorHOUSE®

AuthorHouse™
1663 Liberty Drive
Bloomington, IN 47403
www.authorhouse.com
Phone: 1-800-839-8640

Published by AuthorHouse 11/1/12

ISBN: 978-1-4772-8275-5 (sc)
ISBN: 978-1-4772-8274-8 (e)

Library of Congress Control Number: 2012919773

For Teresa

Contents

INTRODUCTION

My first book of questions was published in 2005 under the title *Ask Me! 728 Questions for Heterosexual and Gay Couples*. As a couples therapist practicing Imago Relationship Therapy, I wrote *Ask Me!* as a resource to enhance my work with couples. This new and improved book of questions, *Just Ask!*, has been expanded to include a section on "This or That," which provides a series of playful but meaningful questions with two clear choices, as well as a section on "Gender," which allows readers to analyze and share their feelings about personal identity and gender. Along with the new categories, existing sections have been expanded to include more questions, adding a total of 272 new questions to this edition.

Another new feature is the table of contents that identifies the question numbers that are associated with each topic. This will assist readers who wish to zero in on a particular topic. For example, if you decide to bring this book to work to do a quick ice-breaker before your morning meeting, you may opt to exclude the questions in the sections on "Romance" and "Sex."

Also new to this book is the "Rescue Dialogue" resource. After many conversations with couples who used this book to deepen their connection, I realized that sometimes conflicts would develop over what was disclosed in answering particular questions. The Rescue Dialogue is a guided script to help you sort through your reactions and make sense of how you jumped the track from inquisitive and interested to hurt and angry. Keep the Rescue Dialogue in mind as you venture curiously into uncharted territories with your question-mate.

Just Ask! is designed to appeal to a diverse audience that extends beyond couples. However, the audience most likely to benefit from using this book the most are those in an intimate relationship who desire to attain a deep and lasting connection through knowing one another well.

What surprised me most about my first book, which I wrote specifically for couples, was how many people enjoyed using the book to ask non-partners many of these same questions. Friends were asking one another questions from the book, and family members too. Soon, it was clear that this is a great way to foster intimacy in all relationships. These questions can lead to surprising, enlightening, enjoyable, thought provoking, and entertaining conversations with just about anyone you know.

While many of the questions in this book assume you have a partner already, there are still many more that do not. Among the other target groups for this book are: family, friends, co-workers, people just starting to date, or engaging in online or long distance relationships, as well as couples who are partnered, married, or otherwise committed. This resource can also be of great help to people who meet and woo potential partners online.

A few years ago, a woman contacted me to offer a quick thank-you for writing *Ask Me!* She explained that she had met her partner on a dating site, and that the two of them each purchased my book and took turns asking one another questions. They did this for a couple of months before ever meeting in person. Eventually they both felt confident enough in their exchanges to meet, and according to her, "the rest is history."

Over the last couple decades of working with couples, I have discovered that many couples with whom I work do not seem to know one another nearly as well as they believe they do. Whether together for one year or twenty years, most couples suffer from the illusion that not only do they know who their partner is, but they also believed they knew how he or she *should* think, feel, be, or act in order to be better! This kind of prescriptive and inaccurate perception, as you might imagine, does not foster warm fuzzies between two people.

Regardless of their motivation for therapy, most couples who seek relationship help share a common concern: feeling disconnected.

Disconnection occurs when we lose the ability to see the world through one another's eyes. We are disconnected when we focus solely on our own needs, wants, hurts, and feelings without regard for our partner. Disconnection is the consequence when we cease to be curious about our partner's thoughts and feelings.

When a couple is disconnected, their complaints may sound like any of the following:

- "He doesn't 'get' me."
- "She wants to change me."
- "Nothing I do is good enough."
- "I am not sure why she stays with me. I don't even think she likes me."
- "We are as opposite as night and day."
- "I just don't get where she is coming from."

We all share a fundamental desire to be known. The process of revealing who we are to another person who reciprocates this sharing is known as intimacy. Intimacy is a word that can be broken into a memorable, helpful, three-word description, *into-me-see*. When you allow others to see into who you are, you are allowing yourself to be known. As simple as it seems, a book of questions is a perfect way to create instant intimacy, and there are many benefits to couples who choose to use a book of questions like this to deepen and refresh their intimacy with each other.

This book will stimulate you to:

- Engage in instant and meaningful conversation.
- Deepen your connection with loved ones.
- Intensify your feelings of desire.
- Think more deeply about who you are, what you believe, and how you feel.
- Increase your intimate sharing.
- Awaken your curiosity.
- Improve your journey.
- Foster more laughter, playfulness, fun, and closeness with those around you.

The questions included in this book give you the opportunity to deepen your connection with anyone in your life. Whether you are sitting in an airport on a three hour delay, taking a ten hour road trip by car, or hiking the Appalachian Mountains by foot, this is a great travel companion for all your adventures great and small. Here's to more curiosity and stronger connection with all the people you care about!

THE POWER OF CURIOSITY

When was the last time you were really curious about someone?

Curiosity is at the heart of connection. Our desire to know, feel close to, and be connected to someone is motivated by pure curiosity. Without it, we are indifferent, disengaged, and uninterested.

Being curious is a form of desire. Reflect on some of your most romantic moments and how you spent them. Chances are that you were intimately engaged with your partner either emotionally, spiritually, physically, or even intellectually. You were likely pursuing a connection that was driven by curiosity mixed with a craving for closeness.

Perhaps you had a longing to curiously explore your loved one's body. Or maybe you took a drive through your partner's childhood neighborhood. You might have gone to her favorite restaurant and tasted all of her favorite foods. Maybe you simply sat in the car holding his hand while his, and possibly now your, favorite song came to its finish. Or was it that you surprised her at work with flowers—the exact flowers you knew she would love because your curiosity drove you to uncover this information?

Romance involves longing, craving, wanting, and desire. Romance is driven by our pursuit to have the object of our desire. Romance is the carriage that is pulled by pure want. It is a means by which we satisfy our senses, our longings, and our desires.

During our initial courtship and dating, we are insatiably curious about our newly found beloved. We have to know more. "What do you do?" "What kind of music do you like?" "Where are you from?" "How long have you been here?" "What's your sign?" Eventually these sweet and innocent questions begin to intensify, changing into questions like, "Do you know how beautiful you are?" and "Where have you been all of my life?" or "Can I kiss you?"

Ultimately we progress to questions like, "How do you feel about monogamy?" Before we know it, we are asking questions like "Do you want kids?" and "Will you move in with me?" and "Will you be my lifetime companion, my partner, my lover, my spouse, my mate?"

And so it is. Until, of course, one day, without any apparent warning or reason, our questions morph into assumptions and statements that sound like "Why are you always late?" or "Am I ever going to be a priority?" and "How can I trust you when you don't do what you say you're going to?" Abracadabra! Poof. Curiosity disappears.

When we stop being curious, we tend to become critical. Here's my mantra. Repeat after me: **Be CURIOUS, not critical.** Repeat after me, "Today I'm going to be curious, not critical!" Now try it. You'll like it, and so will those around you.

When we lose our curiosity about each other, we lose interest. Curiosity feeds interest. Interest feeds desire. When we are critical, we become inclined to think we already know everything there is to know about our partner. In fact, we not only think that we know everything about them, but we even know how to fix what's wrong with them!

We think, or worse yet, say, "If you would only" or "Why don't you," and "Why do you have to_____ when you could _____."

These questions and statements are not examples of curiosity. Instead, these are but a few of the ways we express our criticism. If you hear yourself in these critical statements, don't fret! Curiosity can be replenished. We can reignite the flames of our pure and innocent wonder—the curiosity that guided our hearts right into the arms of our beloved. We can always deepen our connection with the one to whom we are considering committing ourselves, have already committed ourselves, or the one we hope to be with forever.

HOW TO USE THIS BOOK

How you decide to use this resource will depend on your hoped-for outcome. This handy little book of questions can be used for fun and enjoyment, for exploration and getting to know each other, or for reigniting long-lost curiosity. Here are a few strategies I and my readers have found useful in the past:

1.   **Random Picks: Ask your partner to pick a number from 1-1000.** Whatever number your partner picks is the question you will ask him. Once he has answered the question, it is your turn to answer the same question. Next, you pick a number from 1-1000, and your partner will read you the question. You answer the question first, and then your partner does.

2.   **Schedule Time: Set aside 30 minutes a day, every day, asking one another questions out of the book.** Do this in order of 1-1000 until you have completed all 1000 questions in the book. Once you have completed the questions, visit my website at www.micheleomara.com and pick your next relationship resource to continue feeding your relationship and fanning the flames of romance.

3. **Daily Question: Have a "Question of the Day" for 1000 days.** Do the math, and you will see that this fun little adventure can continue providing you with a connection to one another for almost two years!

4. **Travel Companion: Take your book with you when you go on vacations.** Vacations are a great, relaxing way to spend time reacquainting yourself with your partner. Look for a copy of this book in your cabin drawer in romantic bed and breakfasts around the world, cruises, and in the nightstand of your favorite getaway lodges and retreat areas.

5. **Easy Access: Keep a copy of this in your vehicle at all times.** Every time you're stuck in traffic with your partner by your side, pull it out and pick a question.

6. **Coffee Table: Use this book with friends and family.** Keep a copy of this book in a visible place in your home where you regularly socialize with visitors, such as a coffee or end table. When friends and family express interest, invite them to pick a number. Be sure to include a veto policy if the questions picked are too personal to discuss! There are plenty of thought provoking questions to liven up your conversations and turn a casual visit into a great memory.

7. **One-a-Day Commitment: Ask a question a day to someone, anyone.** Take one question per day and commit to yourself that you will find one person every day for the next 1,000 days

to ask each question to—it can be someone you know, someone you want to get to know, or it can even be a stranger. Just ask.

USER GUIDELINES

1. **NEVER answer any question you do not want to answer.** This is called exercising a boundary, and it is a healthy behavior. If you do not feel comfortable discussing something because you are uncomfortable, it feels too personal, or you simply don't want to, then don't.

There is a difference between keeping secrets and maintaining your privacy. With secrets there is shame—a fear of discovery or of something being discovered that you are not at peace with about yourself. Sometimes you will be asked questions that you don't want to answer because you are embarrassed or you fear that you will be judged. Withholding information in these situations can prevent you from having deeper connections because of your fear of being known!

Sometimes, though, it is wise to withhold information from some people because you may not have established a strong enough foundation to know yet what information they can be trusted with and what information they cannot be trusted with. Trust comes from our ability to predict someone's behavior. If you cannot predict how a person will respond to certain information, you may opt to start with the less vulnerable questions and delay sharing the more intimate details of your life until you gain greater clarity about what they will do with the information.

Doing this is called exercising privacy. Maintaining privacy is different from keeping a secret. Privacy is information about yourself that you are not ashamed of, but that you consider personal. Examples of information that people commonly consider private include things related to their personal and intimate relationships (current or past), their medical, legal, financial, or mental health history and experiences.

When you are in a situation where a question is asked that you are not comfortable answering, it is important to set a boundary that may sound as simple as, "I am not comfortable sharing that information," or, "I need to know you better to share that information with you." It is important to know how to confidently set this boundary before engaging in this book of questions. Go ahead and decide on a scripted line that you can count on when you need to set a boundary.

2. **Do not ask a question that you then refuse to answer yourself.** Not nice. Enough said.

3. **Censor questions according to the relationship you have with someone.** For example, you may want to avoid questions about sex when pulling this book out at a family reunion unless, for example, you are truly curious about your grandmother's most erotic sexual fantasy. Yeah, that's what I thought.

4. **Please use this book as a helpful tool, not a hurtful tool.** Do not use the information gained from use of this book to attack, ridicule, or otherwise demean someone. This will lead to a loss of trust in you. To share vulnerable, personal information about who

you really are with someone is a gift. Using this vulnerable information against that person is like throwing a gift back in their face. It can be very hurtful not only to your question partner, but also to the relationship you have with this person.

5. **Address conflicts that arise immediately.** If a question causes a conflict, please go directly to the **RESCUE DIALOGUE** on the next page.

6. **Remain curious, not critical.** The whole purpose of this book is to aid you in deepening your understanding of one another. This is designed to be a fun way to connect. When we are curious, we remain open. When we are critical, we are likely to encounter conflict.

RESCUE DIALOGUE

If you have found yourself in a conflict with someone because the answer to a question caused hurt or angry feelings, use the following Rescue Dialogue to find your way back to a healthy, feel-good connection. This dialogue is adapted from the format used by the Imago Theory called the Intentional Dialogue. This form of communication ensures that both parties to the conversation are heard and that the messages are received accurately.

Reaching an agreement is not the goal, and though it is a good thing when it happens, it's simply not a requirement for effective communication. The goal is to understand one another. The beautiful thing about being human is that we are all unique creatures with unique thoughts, feelings, and experiences. If you desire your friends, family, and significant others to always agree with you and see the world the way you do, then you will likely experience a lot of frustration in life. Accepting our differences and allowing them to exist will lead to greater peace and understanding. Whether you are in agreement with another person or not, make it your intention to understand.

HOW THE RESCUE DIALOGUE WORKS
FIRST: The person with the hurt feelings will be called the SENDER. The sender will start each statement listed below by completing the unfinished portion of

the sentence. Each sentence will be addressed one at a time, allowing the listener to respond.

SECOND: The other person is called the LISTENER. After each statement is finished by the Sender, the Listener will simply repeat what is heard by engaging in the following Listener Response.

THE SENDER'S STATEMENTS

1. When you answered the question the way you did, what I thought was.... (Listener Response—See below for reminder on how to respond.)

2. These thoughts led to a feeling of... (Listener Response)

3. And what hurts me about this is... (Listener Response)

4. What I am afraid of is... (Listener Response)

5. What I imagine you are afraid of about my reaction to your sharing is... (Listener Response)

6. What I hope my reaction to your sharing is able to communicate is... (Listener Response)

7. I hope this because ... (Listener Response)

8. What I need from you to feel safe and secure with our relationship is.... (Listener Response)

9. And what I need to do for myself to feel

more safe and secure in our relationship is....
(Listener Response)

LISTENER RESPONSE

- *"What I heard you say is..."* and verify that you heard what was said accurately.
- Then the Listener will make sure he or she has heard the message accurately by asking the Sender,*"Did I get it?"*
- If the answer is "no," then the Sender will need to clarify the message again for the Listener. The Listener should repeat, or mirror, this clarification from the Sender before proceeding to the next statement.
- Once the Listener has successfully mirrored what the Sender communicated, the Listener will ask: **"Is there more?"** The Sender can then continue with the existing stem statement, or move on to the next one.

THIRD: After all statements have been completed by the Sender and mirrored back and verified for accurate reception by the Listener, then the Listener gets to share his or her feelings with a separate set of stem statements (listed below) that are to be finished.

STATEMENTS TO SENDER

1. When you responded to my answer the way you did, what I thought was... (Sender performs the Listener Response)

2. These thoughts led to a feeling of... (Sender performs the Listener Response)

3. And what hurts me about this is... (Sender performs the Listener Response)

4. What I am afraid of is... (Sender performs the Listener Response)

5. What I understand about your reaction to what I shared that I didn't understand before is... (Sender performs the Listener Response)

6. Knowing how you feel about what I said makes it easier to understand your reaction because... (Sender performs the Listener Response)

7. Understanding how you feel matters to me because... (Sender performs the Listener Response)

8. I want you to feel safe with me because... (Sender performs the Listener Response)

9. What I need in order to feel safe sharing with you in the future is... (Sender performs the Listener Response)

FOURTH: To bring closure to this Rescue Dialogue, each partner will state a closure statement as follows:

1. **SENDER:** I accept your answer as a reflection of who you really are, and I realize that your truth is what it is, whether I am comfortable with it or not. My reaction will not change your truth, and I would rather know your truth and be uncomfortable with it than not know your truth at all. I know that no matter what your truth is, I will be okay.

2. **LISTENER:**I accept your response to my sharing as a reflection of who you are, and I realize that for me to really know you, I have to allow you your feelings, reactions, hurt, anger, or disappointment, even if I am uncomfortable with this. I know that no matter how you respond to who I am, I will still be okay.

THIS BOOK DOES NOT REPLACE THERAPY

If your relationship is in a vulnerable state or you are in turmoil, this is not the ideal tool to address those relationship wounds. This book is not therapy, and it does not replace therapy. Be sure to get proper care and counseling for your relationship, and once you are back on track, get this book out and start asking questions again! This is designed to bring you closer, to offer you opportunities to connect on a deeper level, to provide you with fun and laughter, and to simply serve as a resource to help you know one another better.

If you perceive that your relationship is hanging on by a thread, you will need more than this book of questions to address the problem.

KEEP IT WHERE YOU'LL USE IT

The worst thing you can do with this book is put it on a book shelf. This book is a companion, a relationship aid, and a tool to improve and reenergize your intimate and social connections.

This book offers you at least 1000 great conversation starters and opportunities for connection. If you are a long-term married couple or life partners who are seeking clever ways to reenergize your relationship, this is a great reality check to see if you really do know as much about your significant other as you thought you did!

If you are hanging out with friends and you want something interesting to do, this book is sure to fill the room with a lot of laughter, entertainment, and meaningful conversation. There is so much to learn about everyone you know. Don't be afraid to pull this book out at family gatherings or even among co-workers. You will definitely want to use discretion when choosing questions, and it is useful to remind everyone they do not have to answer anything they do not want to. Have fun with it—let go and learn something new about someone every day.

Your best bet is to put a copy in each car and one in the nightstand next to your bed. Whatever your placement strategy is, just be sure to put this book somewhere that you know you'll use it.

ADD YOUR OWN QUESTIONS!

Do you have questions that should be included in a book like this? Email me at michele@micheleomara.com. I love to hear from my readers!

FAMILY AND CHILDHOOD

1.   Describe yourself as a child. Use at least five adjectives.

2.   When you were a child, how did your family send you to bed and greet you in the morning?

3.   What is your greatest childhood accomplishment?

4.   What did you always want as a child, but never get?

5.   Who was your childhood hero or favorite person (real or imagined), and how did they become so?

6.   Name three of your fondest childhood memories.

7.   Thinking of yourself as a child, which of the following best describes you? 1) lay low and out of the storm, 2) always in trouble, 3) keeping the peace, 4) do my best and make others proud of my achievements, 5) if all else fails, make them laugh.

8.   How would you describe a healthy relationship between an adult child and their

parent? Include frequency of contact, how often you visit, the things you share or don't, how you treat or interact with them, etc.

9. Who was your longest-term best friend as a child, and what's your relationship with them now?

10. What was your favorite childhood story?

11. What is your greatest childhood hurt?

12. Is there something that embarrasses or shames you about your family?

13. Were you teased or made fun of as a child? By whom, how often, and how did you respond? When did it stop and why?

14. Did you tease or mistreat anyone as a child? If so, who and why?

15. How old were you when your parent(s) talked to you about sex, or did they at all?

16. Who was your greatest supporter when you were a child?

17. What was your favorite childhood television program?

18. How did your family spend time together when you were a child?

19. How close is your family to their extended family? Explain any conflicts or disconnects.

20. What are the messages you were given about sex when you were a child?

21. What were your favorite family rituals while growing up? Would you like to continue any of these in your relationship now?

22. Describe your sibling relationships as a child and now.

23. What was your favorite childhood movie?

24. What was your worst physical injury during your childhood?

25. Tell your partner something about your childhood that you've never told another.

26. What brings you the most pride about your family?

27. What are some of your fondest memories of time spent with your family?

28. What is your greatest challenge when it comes to your relationships with your family members?

29. Describe the animals/pets you've kept and what role they played in your life.

30. If you could go back to one time period in your life between the age of 0-18, what year would you choose and why?

31. What messages were you given about homosexuality as a child?

32. If you could erase one year of your life, which would it be and why?

33. Who has most significantly influenced how you became the person you are today? Explain.

34. How did you entertain yourself as a child?

35. How does your family-of-origin handle conflict?

36. Did the important people in your life attend important events in your life?

37. What was the most controversial issue your family-of-origin had to deal with (not including your sexual orientation)?

38. Is there a "boss" in your family-of-origin? If so, who?

39. Who do you most respect in your family-of-origin and why?

40. As a child did you find Barbies, dolls, and playing house more fun, or riding bikes, playing sports, and rough housing?

41. What kind of student were you?

42. Was your family demonstrative, or were your family members reluctant to show their feelings?

43. In your opinion, what's the best thing about being a child?

44. What do you think is the hardest thing about being a child?

45. Do you feel like a grown-up, but still feel separate from your parents' adulthood? If yes, describe when you made this transition. If no, explain.

46. As a child, what were some of the things you thought about while growing up? What did you want to "be" and what kinds of things did you see yourself doing as an adult? How does this compare to what really has unfolded for you as an adult?

47. How did you respond when you didn't get what you wanted as a child? Do you still respond this way as an adult?

48. How did you react to the physical pain of getting hurt as a child? Is this response still the same as an adult?

49. As a child did you prefer to play with other children or animals? Has that changed?

50. As a child did you prefer to spend time with friends, watching TV, or reading a book?

51. Describe your interests as a child.

52. What was your strongest subject in grade school? What was your favorite subject in grade school?

53. Who was your first best friend as a child? When have you last had contact with him/her?

54. Looking at your life through the eyes of yourself as a child, would that child be pleased with who you are today?

55. How was your health as a child? Did you frequently experience health issues?

56. What were you most self-conscious about as a young person?

57. What were you most confident about in yourself as a young person?

58. Did you ever have a crush on a teacher? If you did, how did you behave with him or her?

59. As a child do you remember thinking "if I ever have a child I will never_____?"

60. Did you have any nicknames as a child? What were they and how did they come to be?

61. If you could erase one memory from your childhood, what would it be?

62. If all parents were mandated to learn one new skill as requested by their child, what skill would you have required your parents learn when you were growing up?

63. If you were in charge of where and how your family lived when you were a child, what would have been different?

64. What are three things your parents did that you would never do if you were a parent?

65. What are three things that your parents did that you would be certain to do as a parent?

66. Did you want more or less siblings growing up? Why?

67. Did your parents ever forget your birthday?

68. Did you ever spend more than one whole week out of school when you were a child?

69. What is your favorite summer memory from your childhood?

70. How did your parents treat the topic of pregnancy around you as a child?

FAVORITES

What is your favorite?

71. Vehicle

72. Color

73. Song

74. Movie

75. Meal

76. Holiday

77. Stone

78. Flavor

79. Book

80. Vacation Spot

81. Animal

82. Restaurant

83. Artist

84. Day of the week

85. Fruit

86. Vegetable

87. Meat

88. Soda

89. Dessert

90. Candy

91. Clothing material (Cotton, Silk, Polyester)

92. Flower

93. Time of day

94. Grocery store

95. Alcoholic beverage

96. Non-alcoholic beverage

97. Perfume/cologne

98. Clothing brand

99. Shoes

100. Sport

101. Season

102. Weather

103. Snack food

104. Body part (on your partner)

105. Gum

106. Magazine

107. Temperature/climate

108. TV show

109. Ice cream shop

110. Coffee

111. City

112. Play

113. Concert

114. Person

115. Herb or seasoning

116. Hobby

117. Number

118. Board game

119. Computer/video game

120. Ice cream flavor

121. Female singer

122. Genre of music

123. Male singer

124. Instrument

125. Pastime

126. Language

127. Amusement park

128. Actor

129. Actress

130. Comedian

131. Joke

132. Jewelry

133. Grade school teacher

134. Subject in school

135. College

136. Junk food

137. Web site

138. Baby boy's name

139. Baby girl's name

140. Brand of shampoo

141. Place to have a date

142. Sex position

143. Friend

144. Place to hang out

145. Job that you've had

146. Family member

147. Quote

148. Song lyrics

149. Word

150. Vehicle

151. Place you have lived

HOLIDAYS

152. What is your favorite holiday and how do you like to spend it?

153. With which family and friends have you traditionally spent holidays?

154. What are your expectations of your partner on your birthday and your anniversary?

155. What do you value most about the holidays?

156. What is an ideal birthday celebration for you?

157. Describe the best holiday you can remember.

158. What was your favorite birthday and why?

159. If a national holiday was made in your honor, how would you like to see it celebrated?

160. What are the best and worst holiday gifts you have received throughout your life?

161. Describe how your favorite holiday would unfold if you could be in charge of every detail including with whom (realistic or not) you spend it.

162. What is your ideal anniversary celebration?

163. Do you like to dress in a costume at Halloween? Describe your best and worst costumes over the years.

164. Do you like to decorate your home for some or all holidays? If so, describe how in detail. If not, explain your feelings about why.

165. Are there any major holidays that you don't celebrate? Explain.

166. How do you feel about shopping during the winter holiday season?

167. Are there lapsed holiday rituals or celebrations you experienced as a child that you wish you could incorporate into your adult life?

168. Who are the people that you annually buy presents for including any and all holidays (birthdays, anniversaries, religious holidays, etc.)?

169. What is your typical gift-giving budget for each holiday? Do you usually stick to the budget?

170. If you could only have one or the other, would you rather have a sentimental card or a big expensive gift from your partner?

171. Are you more likely to be done holiday shopping by December 1st or December 24th?

172. Describe your ideal outdoor holiday decorations for each holiday.

173. Are there certain people that you hope to see on certain holidays? If so, which people and what holidays?

HOUSE AND HOME

174. If you had to choose among the following, would you paint your living room walls taupe, light blue, or brick red?

175. If you had your choice of a furniture style, would you choose contemporary, traditional, formal, or rustic?

176. Do you have strong preferences about how laundry is done, folded, and put away?

177. If you and your partner live together, do you want a separate bedroom that you call your own for any reason? Explain.

178. Would you rather invest resources in fixing up the inside or outside of your home?

179. What is your least favorite home-cooked meal?

180. Describe your household cleaning list and how often you like to get each task done.

181. Would you rather live in a ranch or a three story home?

182. If you could live in a cabin in the mountains, a beachfront house on the ocean, a cottage on a lake, an apartment in downtown New

York, a Midwest city somewhere in the suburbs, or in a restored home in an artsy historic district, where would you prefer to live?

183. What do you enjoy the least about household responsibilities?

184. When it comes to the division of labor for a couple, what are your preferred responsibilities around the house? Who should clean, pay bills, care for pets, do lawn care, keep up with maintenance, make repairs, do laundry, cook, clean up dishes, and go grocery shopping? These are just a few of the examples of household responsibilities, so don't feel obligated to stop there!

185. What is the first thing you like to do when you come home from work or time spent away from home?

186. Are you comfortable displaying pictures of you and your partner throughout your home, as well as any other items in your home that may reveal or confirm your relationship?

187. If you could only stock five things in your refrigerator, what would they be?

188. If you could either have a house that is completely clean and dust free but not necessarily organized, or a house in which everything has a place and there is an extreme order but it is not so clean, which would you choose?

189. How do you believe a couple should

determine who gets custody of the TV remote control?

190. What does your dream home look like? You can talk about style, size, location, setting, layout, decoration, etc.

191. Do you have strong feelings about the smell of your home? Explain.

192. How do you feel about cooking? What's your best dish?

193. How much time do you like to spend tending to your garden, flowers, or outdoor landscaping?

194. How often do you like to redecorate your living environment?

195. Who is welcome in your home any time? Who is not?

196. Where do dirty clothes go in your house?

197. Are there any rituals or aids that you require to sleep well at night? Do you use a noisemaker, fans, blinders, darkness, or the like?

198. Who is not welcome in your home without calling first?

199. How long do you want to live where you currently are?

200. If your taste in house decor differs dramatically from your partner's, how would you prefer to address this dilemma?

201. Would you rather have a home-cooked meal or go out to eat? If you prefer a home-cooked meal, would you like to be the one to prepare it or not?

202. If a stereo volume goes from 1-10, at what volume are you most comfortable having it on?

203. If your partner cooked a meal that you did not enjoy, how would you most likely respond?

204. What is the difference between a house and a home to you?

205. When friends and family visit your home, how would you like them to finish this sentence: "Your house is so _____."

206. What skills do you have for home repair, maintenance, or decoration?

207. How do you feel about eating in bed?

208. If a stray animal appears on your back porch one morning, how are you most likely to respond?

209. Would you rather go to someone else's house for dinner or invite them to your place?

210. Do you like having visitors in your house? Describe your feelings about having company.

211. Which is your favorite room in the house?

212. What is your worst habit around the house?

213. What are your pet peeves around the house? Are there certain things that must be done in a particular way?

214. When you are home alone, do you generally have the TV on, radio on, or are you usually in silence? Explain why.

215. Is it important to have a room in your house that you can call your own?

216. In what room of your house do you spend the most time? Explain.

217. If something breaks around your home, would you rather call someone to fix it or figure out how to fix it yourself? Some quick examples include plumbing, panes of glass, furnace, shutter, roof leaks, home appliance malfunction, etc.

218. If you could afford a second home, where would you want it to be located? Where would you want a third home to be located?

219. Describe your bedtime routine. What does the last hour of your day prior to actually going to sleep generally look like? And what time does this routine usually begin?

PERSONAL EXPERIENCES AND WELL-BEING

220. How would you rate your physical health on a scale of 1-10? Ten is "very healthy." How did you arrive at this rating?

221. What is your favorite meal of the day and why?

222. Would you describe your typical energy level as low, average, or high?

223. How many meals do you typically eat each day?

224. Do you frequently diet or restrict your food intake?

225. Are you concerned about your weight? Explain.

226. How many times have you been hospitalized? For what?

227. Do you have any scars? What are the stories that explain them?

228. What is the most consistent positive thing you do to take care of yourself?

229. What is the most irresponsible thing you've ever done?

230. What is the biggest concern in your life right now?

231. What do you most need to do to take care of yourself but often avoid?

232. Have you ever been in a fist fight or brawl with someone? Have you ever physically been aggressive or harmful to a partner or other person you love? If so, describe and include how you felt about it then and feel about it now.

233. The time I remember being most lonely was
    _____.

234. The time I remember being most angry was
    _____.

235. The time I remember being most scared was
    _____.

236. The time I remember being most hurt was
    _____.

237. The time I remember being most joyful was
    _____.

238. What was your greatest accomplishment this month?

239. What are your thoughts about drinking and drug use?

240. What is the most touching experience you have had in the last month?

241. If you had to describe yourself one way or

another, would you say you "live to eat" or "eat to live?"

242. What is more important to you, how you look or how you feel? Explain.

243. What are your views about higher education and its importance in life?

244. Which is more important to you in a mate, personality or intelligence? Why?

245. How do you feel about tattoos? Do you have any? Have you had any removed? Explain.

246. How often do you exercise, and what do you do to support your physical fitness?

247. When, if applicable, is the last time you went on a diet, and what are you like while you're on a diet?

248. How often do you change or modify your eating habits or diet?

249. How much sleep do you require to feel your best? How much sleep do you typically get?

250. What time do you like to go to bed, and what time do you like to wake up?

251. Have you ever witnessed a natural disaster?

252. How, if at all, is your behavior and mood affected by limited sleep, hunger, or (where applicable) PMS?

253. Do you have any routines or patterns that you must adhere to in order to feel centered

or well? For example, do you run every day without fail?

254. How would you describe your appearance to a blind person?

255. Would you ever consider eating dessert and no meal or dessert before your meal?

256. What part of your life needs the most attention in order to create more balance: spiritual, emotional, physical, social, or intellectual? Explain.

257. When did you first experience loss due to a death? What was your most painful experience with death?

258. How has illness in others or yourself affected your life?

259. What are your thoughts about social drinking? How would you describe yourself when it comes to drinking?

BELIEFS AND MORALS

260. Under what, if any, circumstances would you read your partner's journal?

261. If your best friend of many years told you that s/he had always been attracted to you but never had the nerve to deal with it before now, how would you respond?

262. How do you feel about abortion?

263. What are your thoughts about our welfare system?

264. How do you feel about gay marriage? Do you think men should be legally allowed to marry men and women to marry women?

265. Describe your voting habits and thoughts.

266. How do you feel about guns?

267. Which of the following protective responses best describes you: fight, flight, freeze, submit, or play dead? Explain.

268. If your partner didn't want to go to work, and he asked you to call in for him and make up a convincing story about why he will not be there, would you lie for him?

269. How would you describe your political party loyalty and beliefs?

270. Under what, if any, circumstances do you believe it is okay to lie?

271. Do you vote? If so, who was the last president you voted for?

272. If you were on a date with someone who paid the bill but did not tip and your service was good, would you more than likely leave without thinking much about it, feel concerned but not mention it or respond, offer to leave a tip, or would you simply leave a tip on the table once your date was not looking?

273. If your partner experienced a life-changing event that fundamentally changed the kind of person he is in a way that you did not like or approve of, how would you respond?

274. If a co-worker who you work with closely every day shared that she is attracted to you, how would you respond? Would you tell your partner?

275. How true is this statement in your life? "What goes around comes around."

276. How do you feel about assisted suicide (euthanasia)?

277. Do you think that gay men and women who are in positions of influence with other people's children, such as teachers, scout leaders, and child care providers, should

be open about their sexual orientation? Explain.

278. If the cashier gave you back more change than you are owed, how would you respond?

279. What is the biggest lie you ever told? Why and what happened?

280. What advice would you give to yourself ten years ago?

281. What is your view on antidepressants and other mood-stabilizing, nonaddictive medications? Is your opinion about this different for you than for others?

282. If you wanted to adopt a child, would you be willing to deceive the agency in order to improve your chances of a successful adoption?

283. Suppose your friends call you and want you to go to dinner with them, but you are simply tired, not interested, and would rather stay home than go out. Are you more likely to tell them the truth or make up an excuse to prevent them from having hurt feelings?

284. If you saw a child stealing candy in a store, but it appeared as though no one else did, how would you respond?

285. If you and your partner are fighting, and you suspect she is keeping something from you, would you resort to reading her journal to find out what's going on?

286. If you are close friends with both members of another couple, and you learn that one of them is being unfaithful, how would you respond?

287. If you find yourself developing an attraction for someone that your partner doesn't know, how would you handle these unexpected feelings? For example, would you tell your partner, would you discontinue contact with the person if possible, or would you act on your feelings?

288. How would you feel if you learned that as a teenager, your partner contributed to a life that he or she decided to abort?

289. What, if anything, could you learn that would change your entire view of your partner?

290. If you were self-employed and were paid mostly in cash, would you claim all of your income and pay taxes on it?

291. Under what circumstances, if any, would you steal?

292. What is a belief that you have that is probably not shared by the majority of people?

293. If the average lifespan was only 50 years, how would you live your life differently?

294. What are you most grateful for?

295. Would you break the law to save a loved one?

296. How much control do you believe you've had over the course your life has taken?

297. What are three things you would like to change about the world?

298. How old would you say you were if you didn't know your birthdate?

299. If you knew the world was going to end a week from today, how would you spend the next week?

300. Would you be willing to reduce your life expectancy by 10 years if you could spend the rest of your years wealthy?

301. What do you believe will happen to you when you die?

302. Why do you think people climb mountains?

303. Do you believe war is ever justifiable?

304. Do you believe in spanking children?

305. Do you believe in capital punishment?

306. Are we all one?

307. What is wisdom, and how do we gain it?

308. What is your one wish for the world?

309. What is the greatest quality that humans possess?

310. Why aren't more people more happy?

311. What does it mean to live in the now?

312. What prevents people from living to their fullest potential?

313. What would you advocate for if you knew no one would judge you?

SPIRITUALITY AND RELIGION

314. What are you most grateful for in your life?

315. Do you believe in a supreme being?

316. Do you believe in miracles?

317. Have you ever had a near death experience?

318. Have you ever had an experience involving a spirit or someone who is deceased?

319. Do you believe in angels? Explain.

320. Do you believe in heaven and hell?

321. Is it important to you that your partner shares the same religious beliefs? Explain.

322. How do you make sense of your existence in this life? Who or what is your creator? Explain.

323. How do you make sense of death? What do you believe happens to a person upon death?

324. Have you ever been to a psychic? What did she say? Do you believe what you heard?

325. What is the most intense spiritual or religious experience you have ever had?

326. Have you been wounded by religion or spiritual experiences in any way? Explain.

327. How has your relationship, or lack thereof, with a higher power influenced the person you are today?

328. Why do you think bad things happen to good people?

329. Have you ever questioned the existence of God or been angry at God? When and why?

330. What is your religious or spiritual belief about homosexuality?

331. Do you believe that everything happens for a reason, that there is a greater plan for our lives than we are able to see at times?

332. Do you attend church? Why or why not?

333. How do you feel about life after death? What do you believe happens once someone dies?

334. Are you comfortable having a partner who does not share your spiritual or religious beliefs? Could you be with someone whose beliefs are contrary to yours?

335. Do you pray? Expand on this.

336. Would you be comfortable saying a prayer out loud at a meal with friends or family?

337. What are your thoughts about tithing? Do you regularly make financial contributions to a church?

338. Have you ever read the Bible from front to back? What do you think of the Bible? What is your favorite story in the Bible?

339. What are your thoughts about atheism? How do you feel about people who are atheist?

340. What, if any, role do you believe fear should play in religion or spirituality?

341. If reincarnation is an option, and you could return to this life as anything, what would you want to return as?

342. Who or what most shaped your spiritual beliefs? How?

343. If the spiritual health of our nation relied on you to create a spiritual roadmap for the good of all people, what would your roadmap suggest that people do?

344. Why do you think there is poverty and suffering in the world?

345. What is the greatest gift you have offered this world?

346. What is the meaning of life?

347. What is the relationship between poverty and suffering in the world?

348. Is religion today serving its purpose?

QUIRKS AND PREFERENCES

349. Are there textures, scents, or sensations that you cannot tolerate?

350. Is good grammar important to you in your mate selection? Explain.

351. In your opinion, do most clothes, including jeans, need to be ironed before being worn? Explain.

352. Do you read the newspaper? Which one(s) and how often?

353. What is your favorite news source, be it a news station, magazine, radio, program, or anything else?

354. Do you keep a journal? If you were to title a journal of your thoughts, what would the title be and why?

355. Do you have a birthmark? Where?

356. Are you superstitious about anything?

357. How do you feel about being an organ donor?

358. Describe how you would like your funeral service to be.

359. Do you nap? If you nap, where do you usually nap, for how long, how often, and what time of the day?

360. Which side of the bed do you prefer? What's a good solution if both you and your partner prefer the same side?

361. Do you have any routines or behaviors that you engage in every day that many others do not?

362. What are your thoughts about bumper stickers?

363. How do you feel about having your picture taken?

364. Which section of the video store are you most likely to go to first? What type (Drama, Comedy, Action, etc.) of video are you most likely to leave with, and how many will you rent at once?

365. When you read a book, do you always read from cover to cover, or do you sometimes skim or skip sections, jump around, or read the ending first?

366. Do you prefer certain condiments when you sit down to a meal? Is ketchup, salt, pepper, hot sauce, or anything similar a must-have at mealtimes for you?

367. How do you respond when you are dining in the home of friends or family and you are presented with a meal you do not like?

368. How do you feel about eating meat?

369. Are you inclined to double check that doors are locked, stoves are off, and irons and toasters are not plugged in?

370. What is your most quirky or unusual behavior?

371. Do you have a preference for how the leading edge of toilet paper is directed on the roll?

372. If you had the opportunity, would you want to go to the moon?

373. Have you ever picked up a hitchhiker? How do you feel about hitchhiking?

374. How do you feel about homeless people? Are you likely to offer money to someone requesting handouts?

375. Describe your sleep habits. How many pillows do you use at night? Do you snore? Are you a light or heavy sleeper?

376. Are you more often cold or hot?

377. Do you like shopping? What kind and for how long?

378. What is the average length of time you spend in the shower or bath?

379. What are your thoughts about opening doors for others? Do you feel the same about it for women as you do men?

380. Do you prefer to drive or ride as a passenger with friends and family?

381. If you are lost, do you ask for directions?

382. Are there any modes of transportation you are not comfortable with?

383. How do you feel about having a TV in the bedroom?

384. What's your favorite section of the bookstore or library?

385. How do you feel about rain and snow?

386. How do you feel about gum chewing?

387. How much "alone time" do you need? What happens if you don't get it?

388. What is the most aggravating sound to you?

389. What is the most irritating sight to you?

390. What is the most disgusting taste to you?

391. Is there a way of being touched that makes you cringe?

392. What is the most repulsive smell to you?

393. Will you kiss someone with smoker's breath?

394. Will you kiss someone with alcohol on their breath?

395. When you think about the most

uncomfortable situations you've ever been in, what do you think of first?

COMMUNICATION

396. Would you rather hear words of affection or receive a hand-written note or card?

397. How often do you like to hear the words, "I love you?" How often do you feel comfortable saying them? Explain.

398. When someone you care about is upset, are you more inclined to comfort and nurture or to work to fix the problem for them? Explain.

399. Would you rather have your partner wash your car or bring you flowers?

400. Would you rather spend time in the house doing your own thing or spend time doing something together with your partner?

401. If you and your partner have an argument, what do you like to do when it's over?

402. What is the most difficult thing for you to talk about? Why?

403. What does your partner do or say that causes you the most discomfort when you are alone? And when you are in public?

404. If your partner could only use one method

to communicate his feelings to you, which would you prefer:

- Acts of service (doing things for you to show his love);
- Quality time spent together (being close to you as much as possible);
- Physical contact / touch;
- Receiving gifts; or
- Verbal words of affirmation and affection?

405. If you have a problem, who are you most likely to turn to?

406. What is your most common tactic used to avoid doing something?

407. Describe what your partner's voice sounds like to you and how hearing it makes you feel.

408. What, more than anything else, communicates to you that someone loves you?

409. What frustrates you most about how your partner communicates?

410. What do you appreciate most about how your partner communicates?

411. How lovable do you consider yourself to be on a scale of 1-10, ten being the most lovable ever?

412. Would you rather fight about, discuss, or avoid painful situations? Explain.

413. When your feelings are hurt or you feel angry,

are you more likely to verbally explode or withdraw into silence? Explain this.

414. Do you consider yourself a good communicator? Explain.

415. What behaviors do you engage in to avoid a fight with a friend, partner, or important other in your life?

416. Some people say that communication is the key to successful relationships. Do you agree? Explain.

417. How are you most likely to behave if you suspect something you've done will make your partner angry, but you want to keep her from getting upset?

418. How do you behave when you feel guilty?

419. What is the best way for your partner to get your attention?

420. Do you have a need that you suspect your partner will never be able to meet?

INTIMATE RELATIONSHIPS

421. What three characteristics do you most love about your partner?

422. What are five adjectives you would use to describe your partner? Of those, which are you most proud?

423. What are the first three things that come to mind when you consider what a "perfect" relationship looks like to you?

424. Good partners will always _____ and never _____.

425. What do you least like about your partner's family?

426. If you could ensure one constant characteristic in your partner, which of the following would you choose? Funny, smart, or honest?

427. What attracted you to your partner first?

428. How do you know when a relationship is in trouble? If you saw this signal, how would you respond?

429. What's more important to a relationship— honesty or kindness?

430. Are you comfortable with and/or willing to go to bed mad at your partner? If you are willing to go to bed mad, are you likely to do so on the couch or in bed with your partner?

431. Do you want a relationship commitment event such as a ceremony, wedding, or domestic partnership? Explain.

432. If your partner said he wanted to commit to you, but couldn't promise you "forever," would that affect your decision to commit to him?

433. What three character traits about your partner do you value most?

434. If you have had a relationship commitment event, describe how you feel about how it went. If you have not had one, describe what you would like, or explain why you don't want one.

435. Do you want children? If yes, how many and when? Do you want to adopt, give birth, use a surrogate, and to what extent are you willing to go to include children in your family (expense, use of fertility treatment, etc.)?

436. When it comes to how you relate to your partner, are you more dominant or submissive? Explain.

437. If you could forbid three things from occurring in your relationship, what would they be?

438. Are you still in contact with any of your ex-partners? If so, how often do you get in touch, and how do you feel about them now?

439. Have you ever experienced unrequited love? With whom?

440. Once you make a commitment to a partner—a lifetime commitment, be that through a ceremony, a wedding or other formal and stated commitment—do you believe that the loss of attraction or loss of passion is sufficient reason to separate?

441. How long do you believe passion lasts in the average relationship? Explain.

442. If your partner has a work party and he is not "out" about your relationship to his coworkers, would you expect him to take you anyway, skip the party all together, or go alone?

443. How important is it to you to have a partner who is intelligent?

444. Would your attraction to your partner change if s/he lost or gained weight?

445. Are there any behaviors or characteristics about a potential partner that automatically rule them out? What are they?

446. You know you are in love when _____.

447. Starting with most important to least

important, how would you prioritize passion, commitment, and friendship when it comes to a relationship?

448. What are you most passionate about when it comes to your own interests?

449. Are there any commitments you have made to yourself that you are unwilling to compromise?

450. After committing to a partner—stating your intention to be together FOREVER—what, if anything, do you think justifies changing that commitment at a later date?

451. Do you believe that love and attraction feel the same at the beginning of a relationship as they do after 5, 10, 15, 20, 30, 50, and 70 years together? Explain how you view love's evolution or changes if you believe that it does.

452. What do you consider appropriate to discuss about an ex with your partner? What is absolutely not appropriate to discuss?

453. How do you feel about couples taking separate vacations?

454. Do you believe that most couples who commit to each other remain in love? If not, how do you make sense of why some people seem to fall out of love?

455. Do you consider sexual fantasy about others a form of infidelity? Is there anyone

in particular you would not want your partner to fantasize about?

456. What did you believe you could change about your partner when you first met? Did you?

457. In your lifetime, have you ever been unfaithful to a partner?

458. Are you okay with your partner flirting with others? Explain.

459. What three things do you hope will never happen in your relationship?

460. What defines "family" to you?

461. If you could restart your relationship with your partner, what would you do differently?

462. What are your partner's top three complaints about you? If you were willing to work on only one of them, which would you choose and why?

463. What is your greatest fear about committing to a relationship for life?

464. What do you consider to be the biggest drawbacks associated with being in a long-term relationship?

465. What is the best part of being in a relationship for you?

466. What is your favorite term of endearment that your partner uses for you? What is your

favorite term of endearment you use to refer to your partner?

467. What do you fear you might miss out on if you are in a long term relationship?

468. What are three of the most important things you've learned from your partner?

469. How long would you like this relationship to last?

470. If you learned information that confirmed that your partner is having an affair, how would you respond?

471. If you inadvertently discovered your partner's email password, would you let your partner know so that she had the option to change it, or would you keep that information "just in case" you needed it someday?

472. What is the single greatest strength you have to offer in a relationship?

473. What worried/worries you most about introducing your partner to your family?

474. What do you respect most about your partner?

475. What do you consider your partner's most endearing quality?

476. When did you know you were attracted to people of the same or opposite-sex?

477. When and with whom was your first kiss?

478. When your partner looks at you, what do you most commonly think he or she is thinking?

479. How would you react if your partner told you s/he wanted a sex change?

480. What is your most preferred form of affection?

481. Are there any circumstances in which you would feel comfortable serving as an egg or sperm donor? If so, describe. How do you feel about your partner being a donor?

482. What is the single most important characteristic in a person?

483. If you had to choose between a relationship that was full of excitement, passion, chaos, and conflict or one that is stable, reliable, predictable, and calm, which would you prefer and why?

484. Who is your least favorite person to visit because you feel obligated?

485. If your grandparents are about to celebrate their 50th wedding anniversary with all of your family planning to be in attendance, and you are expected to spend the entire weekend out of town celebrating with them, but it happens to conflict with your partner's recognition ceremony for a major accomplishment she has made at work (or substitute any significant event that will not be repeated), which event do you attend? Explain.

486. Would you be willing to die for anyone? If so, who?

487. What is your least favorite outfit or clothing item that you've seen your partner in?

488. What is the biggest relationship mistake you've ever made, and how did it change you?

489. What first attracted you to your partner and why? How has that changed since then?

490. What is the ultimate goal of being partnered for you? Does your relationship support your idea of the highest good of partnership?

491. What is the worst thing you can imagine happening in a long-term, committed relationship?

492. If your love and attraction to your partner was unequal, would you rather be the one who is more attracted to your partner or the reverse?

493. Do you believe in soul mates? Explain.

494. If your partner develops a crush on someone, do you believe that is an indication that she is no longer in love with you? (A helpful hint: be sure you use the word "crush" the same way).

495. What is the difference between love and "in-love?"

496. Do you believe that a same-sex couple must

have a ceremony or commitment in order to establish the same level of commitment that a heterosexual couple does by marrying? Explain.

497. What do you hope never changes about your partner?

498. What do you wish you could change about your partner?

499. What is one key lesson you have learned about yourself from a prior relationship?

500. Of all of your prior relationships, which one hurt you most deeply? How?

501. Of all of your prior relationships, which one taught you the most about yourself? What was the lesson?

502. What do all of your prior relationships have in common?

503. What is the biggest relationship mistake you have ever made, and how do you feel about that today?

504. How are love and being in a relationship different than you always thought they would be?

505. What's the best thing about being in a relationship?

506. What's the hardest thing about being in a relationship?

507. Do you believe same-sex couples have the

same capacity for long-term relationships as heterosexual couples?

508. Do you believe that real love requires personal sacrifice? Explain.

509. What's the best reason you can think of to commit yourself to a relationship with just one other person for the rest of your life?

510. Which of the following adjectives best describes how you see yourself as a partner: jealous, aloof, preoccupied, needy, emotional, intense, or playful? Which will your partner say best describes you?

511. Describe your first impression of your partner.

512. Would you agree to a marital contract that specified that neither partner can gain or lose more than 10 pounds?

513. How do you feel about your partner maintaining a friendship with his or her ex partner(s)?

514. What are your top three relationship deal-breakers?

ROMANCE

515. What is your idea of a romantic evening?

516. Do you believe in destiny?

517. Is romance important to you? Explain.

518. Upon receiving flowers, are you more inclined to think, "these are too expensive and they will just die," or are you more likely to think, "how sweet and thoughtful, I love these!"?

519. What is the most romantic song you have ever heard?

520. How would you describe the way love feels?

521. If you could only have one, would you rather have a commitment or romance?

522. How would you define the word romance?

523. If you were to write an instruction manual about how to effectively romance you, what are some must-haves for this manual?

524. How important is foreplay to you?

525. How much time do you believe it takes to truly know you are in love?

526. Do you consider yourself a romantic?

527. What is your opinion about love at first sight?

528. Do you like to mix alcohol and romance?

529. What is your favorite love scene of all time from either a book or a movie? Describe it.

530. What's the most romantic outfit you have seen your partner wear?

531. What is the most romantic gesture you have ever seen, heard of, or read about?

532. What is commonly considered romantic that you do not like?

533. What is your idea of a perfect date?

534. What is the difference between sexuality and sensuality?

535. Describe the difference between having sex and making love.

536. What is the most romantic thing you've ever done?

537. Who has given you the best relationship advice, and what was it?

538. When you are attracted to someone, what do you hope they will notice first about you?

SEXUAL ORIENTATION

539. What do you think determines a person's sexual orientation? How does someone become heterosexual, bisexual, or gay?

540. What, if any, stereotypes of gays do you believe apply to you?

541. If you could have a conversation with your creator, how do you think your creator would answer the question, "Why are some people gay?"

542. Would you read a book with "gay" in the title where passersby can see it, as would be the case in a public venue such as a book store or coffee shop?

543. Are you comfortable being in public with friends who fit stereotypes and are likely to be assumed to be gay by strangers?

544. If you could take a pill today to ensure that all future attractions you experience from today forward are to the opposite gender of your current attractions, would you? Explain your response.

545. What word do you like your partner to use to refer to you? For example, wife, partner, lover,

girlfriend, husband, boyfriend, significant other, etc. (Or perhaps paramour, swain, mistress, sweetheart, or inamorato are more you liking)?

546. Who is the first person you met or heard of that you knew was gay?

547. How did your family talk about or treat gay people?

548. Do you believe in the legalization of same-sex marriages?

549. Do you believe homosexuality is a sin?

550. Did your family have close friends or family members who were gay? If so, how were these people treated by your family?

551. What is the best thing about your sexual orientation, be it gay, bisexual, heterosexual, or other?

552. What do you consider the worst thing about your sexual orientation?

553. How do you think others feel about your sexual orientation?

554. How important is it to you that people not make assumptions about your sexual orientation?

555. Describe how you think your life path may have been different if you came into the world with a different sexual orientation?

556. What do you think about bisexuality?

557. Do your feelings about female homosexuality differ from your feelings about male homosexuality?

558. Do you think it is healthy for children to be born or adopted into a family of gay or lesbian parents? Explain.

559. How do you see yourself as fitting, or not fitting, stereotypes of gay men and lesbians? For example, on a scale of 1-10, 1 being completely feminine and 10 being completely masculine, how would you rate your gender appearance, which includes dress, mannerisms, body language, voice, and so on?

560. How important is it to you to be "out" about your sexual orientation and your relationship?

561. What has been the most hurtful experience you have had that is directly related to your sexual orientation?

562. At what age were you aware of your sexual orientation?

563. Did you ever go through a period of exploration around your sexual orientation?

564. Have you ever been mistaken for the wrong sexual orientation? How did you respond?

GENDER

565. How do you feel about the gender you were assigned at birth (male / female)?

566. Do you feel comfortable in men's clothes, women's clothes, or both?

567. Is there anything that you wish you could do that your gender limits you from doing?

568. Is there anything you envy about the other gender?

569. What pleases you most about being the gender you are?

570. Do you ever wish you were born the other gender?

571. How would you feel if you had a child who wanted to change his or her gender?

572. Have you ever met someone who is transgender or transsexual?

573. What is the most enviable thing about being a male?

574. What is the most enviable thing about being a female?

575. If you had to swap any part of your body with someone of the other gender, what would it be, and why?

576. If you were the other gender, what would you want your name to be?

577. Do you ever fantasize that you have the anatomy of the other gender?

578. What do you find most appealing about men and about women?

579. What is the best thing about being a man and the best thing about being a woman?

SEX

580. Have you always practiced safe sex with your partners? How do you define "safe sex?"

581. How long do you like to remain close to your partner (in bed or wherever you are!) after you have concluded a sexual activity? What do you like to do during that time?

582. What are your thoughts about masturbation? How do your opinions differ about masturbation for someone single verses partnered?

583. When it comes to genital hair, do you prefer the area to be shaved or unshaved?

584. Have you been tested for HIV? When? Why were you tested? What were the results?

585. When did you have your first orgasm?

586. How do you feel about anal sex?

587. What's your favorite sexual activity?

588. Do you enjoy any pain associated with sexual pleasure? Describe.

589. If your partner wants to be sexual and you

do not, are you comfortable telling him/her "no?"

590. Would you be willing to be tied, bound, or otherwise restrained during sex with your partner?

591. How would your partner know if you wanted to have sex with him?

592. What are the three most sensitive/sensual parts of your body?

593. Would you be willing to role-play for your partner if he or she asked?

594. Do you want to know when or if your partner masturbates?

595. Describe your most erotic sexual fantasy.

596. How is your view of sex different now that you are an adult than it was as an adolescent?

597. If you knew it was a turn-on for your partner, would you be comfortable with his or her cross-dressing during sex?

598. What's the difference between sexy and erotic?

599. What's the most outrageous place you would like to have sex?

600. Do you prefer to shower with or without the company of your partner?

601. How many sexual partners have you had?

602. What have you never tried sexually but would like to?

603. What percentage of your sexual fantasies involves men and what percentage involves women? How do you feel about each?

604. Describe your ideal environment for lovemaking. Include where you are, what your environment looks like, smells like, feels like, and how long you spend there.

605. Identify ten activities that you consider sensual, not necessarily sexual, such as a back rub, holding hands, cuddling, kissing, caressing, rubbing feet, cooking a meal for your partner, having a conversation, looking one another in the eyes lovingly, etc.

606. How do you feel about oral sex, both giving and receiving?

607. What do you enjoy seeing your partner wear prior to, or during, a sexual encounter together?

608. Do you have any fetishes? What are they?

609. How do you feel about penetration? For males and females, address giving and receiving anal penetration, and for females, additionally address giving and receiving vaginal penetration.

610. How do you feel about role-playing while being sexual?

611. What is the most erotic scent to you? Erotic

taste? Erotic texture? Think silk, soft skin, chocolate syrup—whatever.

612. How important is hygiene to you during sexual contact? For example, is it important to you to be freshly showered or to have your partner freshen up prior to love making?

613. How would you feel if your partner had no sex drive, but was willing to be sexual with you in order to please and meet your needs?

614. Do you believe it's important to continue having sex on a regular basis even if both partners are no longer interested?

615. How would you respond if your partner who has always been interested in having sex suddenly stopped wanting to be sexual?

616. If your partner asked you whether or not you were willing to engage in a threesome with another person, how would you respond? If yes, what genders would you want involved?

617. If your partner suggested that you consider making your relationship "open" to allow both of you to see other people but remain committed to one another, what would your reaction be?

618. How do you feel about mixing sexual activity and sex toys, food, oils, games, lubricants, and other sexual aids? Explain.

619. What are you absolutely unwilling to explore or do sexually?

620. Do your sexual fantasies include members of either gender, or one more than the other?

621. How would you describe a "quickie" when it comes to having sex? What are you thoughts about quickies?

622. Is there a place, in public or private, where you would like to have a sexual rendezvous with your partner? If yes, where?

623. Describe your feelings about male genitals? What about female genitals?

624. Would you rather give or receive sexual attention and why?

625. How do you feel about public displays of affection?

626. Have you ever had a sexually transmitted disease? Have you been sexual with people known to have STDs?

627. How important is breast size, or penis size, to you?

628. What body part do you consider the biggest turn on?

629. Do you have a favorite time of the day to be sexual? How about a least favorite time?

630. How much time is too much to go without sex?

631. What is the biggest sexual turn off for you?

HAVE YOU DONE, OR ARE YOU WILLING TO TRY, THE FOLLOWING?

632. Record sex with your partner on video for personal use?

633. Kiss a woman?

634. Kiss a man?

635. Be awakened by sexual touch in the middle of the night?

636. Have your partner look at and explore your genitals?

637. Have your partner trim or shave your pubic hair?

638. Trim or shave your partner's pubic hair?

639. Have anal sex?

640. Wrestle or "play fight" in a sexual way?

641. Have chest, breasts, nipples rubbed?

642. Give oral sex?

643. Receive oral sex?

644. Have a threesome?

645. Have phone sex?

646. Give oral anal sex?

647. Receive oral anal sex?

648. Masturbate in a car or public place (restroom, theatre, etc)?

649. Use a vibrator?

650. Use a strap-on with a partner?

651. Be tied up?

652. Tie someone up?

653. Give hand job / clitoral finger/ hand stimulation?

654. Receive hand job / clitoral finger / hand stimulation?

655. Have sex in a public space?

656. Be a voyeur by watching others have sex?

657. Have sex in a car?

658. Receive anal penetration (penis or toy)?

659. Give anal penetration (penis or toy)?

660. Have sex at a drive-in?

661. Join the mile-high club (have sex in an airplane)?

662. Have sex with a stranger?

663. Have a one night stand?

664. Have sex in water?

665. Pinch or have any kind of clamp used on your body during sex?

666. Pinch a partner or have any kind of clamp used on his or her body during sex?

667. Scratch a partner?

668. Be scratched by a partner?

669. Bite a partner?

670. Be bitten by a partner?

671. Have sex naked with lights on?

672. Have sex naked with lights off?

673. Be a submissive to someone?

674. Have sex with clothes on?

675. Communicate sexual fantasy to /with a partner?

676. Request of your partner to continue after having an orgasm?

677. Masturbate in front of, or simultaneously with, your partner?

678. Make noise while you have sex?

679. Seduce your partner all day via phone, email and text while apart?

680. Have cyber sex in a chatroom?

681. Send sexual images to your partner via email or text?

682. Engage in sexual activity while menstruating?

683. Have a partner read you erotica?

684. Moan loudly during an orgasm?

685. Read your partner erotica?

686. Have a partner ejaculate on you, female ejaculation included?

687. Receive a light spanking?

688. Give a light spanking?

689. Read erotica?

690. Give hickeys?

691. Receive hickeys?

692. Play strip poker or other game with friends?

693. Have sex in the shower?

694. Have sex standing up against a wall?

695. Have sex without kissing?

696. Watch porn together?

697. Watch porn alone?

698. Use blindfolds with sex?

699. Tickling your partner?

700. Be tickled by your partner?

701. Dry hump (frottage) your body against your partner's?

702. Scissor or rub your naked genitals together with your partner's (tribadism)?

703. Use ice sexually?

704. Roleplay sexually?

705. Use whipped cream or other foods during sex?

706. Have sex with someone much older than you?

707. Have sex with someone much younger (but of legal age!)?

708. Have sex in the ocean while people swim all around you?

709. Have silent sex in a house full of people?

ALL ABOUT YOU

710. When you are upset or sad, how do you like to be comforted?

711. Is your glass half empty or half full?

712. What about yourself do you find most attractive?

713. When was the last time you cried, and what were the circumstances?

714. How would you prioritize the following in your life? Physical health, love, financial security, emotional stability, intellectual capacity, spiritual connectedness, and pleasure?

715. If you had to surrender one of your senses, would you choose to do without smell, taste, touch, hearing, or sight? Explain.

716. If your city was about to be hit by a natural disaster, and you had 48 hours to evacuate, what, if any, possessions would you refuse to leave without?

717. What is the greatest dream you have fulfilled so far in your life?

718. If you could be a contestant on a game show, what game show would you choose?

719. If you had to spend an entire year on an island, and you could take only one person and 5 possessions, who and what would you take?

720. Would you consider yourself a team player or more of a do-it-alone kind of person?

721. What about your personality would you most like to change and why?

722. If you are awakened in the night, is it difficult to get back to sleep?

723. How important is it to you to be on time?

724. If you could have a lunch date with any person alive or dead, who would you pick and why?

725. What is the most important material item you hope to acquire in this lifetime?

726. At what age would you like to retire, and how would you like to spend the years of your retirement?

727. When you reflect on the person you are today, do you feel at peace with how you live and who you are? If not, what are some of the areas you would like to improve or change?

728. If you were partnered with a successful, very visible person who was sought after by many,

would you enjoy their success or feel threatened by it?

729. In detail, describe how you would like your life to look in five years. Think about the personal, professional, social, spiritual, and intellectual areas of your life.

730. Fast forward 20 years. What do you envision your life will look like?

731. On a scale of 1-10 with 10 being the most confident, how confident do you feel about your ability to create a life that fits with what you want for yourself?

732. Describe one desire or wish you have that most people don't know about you.

733. Would you rather speak to a group of 100 or 10?

734. Do you like surprises? What was your best surprise?

735. How do you feel about aging and people knowing how old you are?

736. Would you rather vacuum or clean the bathroom?

737. What is your most embarrassing experience?

738. Do you prefer to text or call someone?

739. How much time per day do you spend playing online games or video games?

740. How would you describe your tolerance for diversity, including race, religion, socioeconomic status, gender expression, etc.?

741. Do you consider yourself a morning or a night person?

742. How important is music to you? Describe.

743. If you could experience only one of the following, which would you choose and why? Going to the moon, being president, starring in a Hollywood production with the cast and directors of your choice, hosting your own talk show, making a life-changing discovery, inventing a culture-changing product or service, or winning an Olympic sport?

744. How do you believe our world has been affected by online social networks such as Facebook?

745. On a scale of 1-10 with 10 meaning "very competitive," how competitive would you say you are?

746. What is the best compliment you have received in the last month?

747. If you could magically play any musical instrument you wanted, what instrument would you choose?

748. What has the greatest influence on your decision making process about what you consider is "right" and what is "wrong?"

749. What are three reasons you believe other people like you?

750. What's the difference between self-confidence and bragging? Explain.

751. What are you most likely to get teased about? What are you most likely to tease your partner about? Are there any subjects about which you don't wish to be teased?

752. Have you ever meditated? Describe.

753. What's the most shocking thing you've ever witnessed?

754. What do you daydream about?

755. Which would you rather hear: children laughing, a cat meowing, the low hum of conversation in the background at a coffee shop, cheering at a sporting event, or silence?

756. What's the first thing you usually do when you wake up?

757. What does an ideal Saturday look like to you?

758. What types of books did you read as a child?

759. Do you know any magic tricks?

760. Which would you pick if you had to do one of the following in front of a large audience: sing, dance, stand up comedy, acting, play an instrument, or read poetry?

761. What, if anything, has caused you to cry happy tears?

762. What are ten things that bring you joy?

763. When was the last time you cried, and why?

764. When was the last time you laughed so hard you weren't sure you could stop?

765. Who is the most real person you have ever known?

766. What is the biggest risk you've ever taken? How did it go?

767. How much time per day do you spend on the computer?

768. How much of the time you spend on the computer is for work, and how much of it is recreational?

769. What is your favorite month of the year? Why?

770. When you share a frustration with your partner, what is an ideal way for him to respond?

771. How would you describe your sense of humor?

772. Do you have a lucky number? What is it?

773. If you were a color, what would you be and why?

774. When you are sad, how will your partner know?

775. What is the single greatest thing about who you are?

776. What is the biggest mistake you've ever made?

777. Have you ever stalked (calling, following, writing, emailing, etc.) someone? Describe the circumstances and frequency of this behavior.

778. When is the last time you lost your temper? Explain.

779. What are three of your pet peeves?

780. If you were stuck in one emotion for an entire week without a break, would you rather be stuck in anger, fear, guilt, or sadness?

781. If you discovered your partner was secretly using cocaine while away on business trips, how would you respond?

782. Are you a cigarette smoker? What are your feelings about having a partner who smokes? Explain.

783. Describe the happiest moment you can recall ever experiencing.

784. Are there things about you that you consider quirky or eccentric? Describe.

785. When you aren't feeling well, such as when

you have a cold, how do you like to be treated?

786. Describe how it feels to you to be sad.

787. Do you enjoy playing board games? Which games do you most enjoy? Which is your least favorite?

788. Have you ever experienced a natural disaster?

789. How do you feel about apologizing and apologies?

790. When do you feel most at peace in your life?

791. What are the things you are grateful for in your life right now?

792. Would you describe yourself as an outdoors person? Explain.

793. If you had short notice of immediate danger to your home, and you had time enough to grab three things before leaving before everything else would be destroyed by a natural disaster, what items you would take with you? (Note, there are no people or pets in your home to consider).

794. What is the most difficult feeling for you to express?

795. When is the last time you felt joyful?

796. How many times on average would you say you laugh per day?

797. When is the last time you cried? What triggered the tears?

798. If you are at a sad movie and you begin to feel tears well up, do you allow yourself to cry or do you stuff your feelings?

799. What do you fear most in life?

800. What were some of the unspoken rules about feelings in your family when you were growing up? For example, was it okay to express anger, sadness, and fear?

801. What are your thoughts and feelings about suicide?

802. What do you believe is your purpose in life?

803. If you could have access to three people at all times, living or not, to help you make decisions, who would you choose?

804. What inspires you? Who inspires you?

805. If this year were your last, how would you choose to spend it?

806. How would you describe your temper?

807. How would your best friend describe you? List at least five adjectives.

808. How would your mother describe you? List at least five adjectives.

809. Describe a song, movie, performance, work

of art, or other visual or auditory experience that moved you to tears.

810. How would an ex-partner describe you? List at least five adjectives.

811. Do you consider yourself an introvert, an extrovert, or somewhere in between?

812. If you have a choice between going to a party with all of your closest friends and staying home with your loved one to watch a movie, which would you prefer?

813. Finish this sentence: "If I never had to work again, I would spend my time…"

814. What would you have the most difficulty accepting about someone you love?

815. Complete the sentence… "I hope _____"

816. Complete the sentence… " I want _____"

817. Complete the sentence… "I resent_____"

818. Complete the sentence… "I know _____"

819. Complete the sentence… "I believe _____"

820. Complete the sentence… "I appreciate ___"

821. Complete the sentence… "I regret _____"

822. Complete the sentence… "I love _____"

823. If you could pick anyone as your mentor, who would it be and why?

824. What would you title the autobiography of your life?

825. What songs would be included on the soundtrack to your life?

826. What is your least favorite activity ever?

827. What celebrity are you most likely to be mistaken for?

828. Have you ever felt like you were on the TV show, *Candid Camera*? Explain.

829. What is your greatest distraction?

FRIENDS

830. If you knew your friends would disapprove of a person you were interested in dating, would you let that affect your decision to ask him or her out?

831. If you could have one best friend who was completely trustworthy and always there for you or 15 fun, interesting, and sometimes unreliable friends, which would you choose?

832. What are the top three most irritating behaviors you have endured while living with friends or family?

833. How important is it to you to have a diverse set of friends who represent different races, cultures, sexual orientations, religious beliefs, and the like?

834. Who do you know better than anyone else, not including your partner?

835. What is your preferred mode of communication with long distance friends? How often do you like to be in communication with them?

836. Who do you correspond with by phone, email, US mail, or in person on a regular basis?

837. If your partner had a job opportunity in another city that would significantly improve the quality of your financial life, would you move away with him or her and lose regular contact with your friends?

838. Who is your best friend and why?

839. How comfortable would you be sharing your answers to these questions with your friends? Does it depend on the subject matter of the question?

840. Do you need alone time with your friends that does not include your partner? Explain.

841. What topics, if any, do you NOT want your partner to ever discuss with friends?

842. Who knows you better than anyone else in the world right now?

843. What characteristics do you look for in potential friends?

844. Have you ever been hurt by a close friend? What happened?

845. If you had a best friend that criticized your partner and refused to spend time with the two of you together, how would you respond to the friend?

846. What behaviors do you consider unacceptable between friends? Provide examples, not suggestions! To help you think of answers, consider ideas like friends should not talk more intimately than my partner and I,

friends should not sleep in the same bed, friends should not need "alone" time without me present, etc.

847. Have you ever betrayed a close friend? How?

848. Who is your longest-term friend, and how do you think you've maintained this friendship for so long?

WORK

849. If you had an opportunity to secure a desirable work account or a much-sought-after position or project, but to do so you had to forego the celebration of your partner's long-planned birthday, which choice would you make?

850. Are there any occupations that you consider off-limits for your partner? If so, what are they?

851. Are you willing to move for your job? For your partner's job?

852. What is the most challenging job you've ever had?

853. As a child, what did you want to be when you grew up? If you are not that now, what changed?

854. What do you want to be sure you achieve before your life's end?

855. Would you describe yourself as a loyal employer or employee? If so, why?

856. What's more important to you, having a

deeply satisfying work life or having a deeply satisfying relationship?

857. If someone offered you $100,000 to pose for nude photographs to be run in a local publication, would you?

858. What was the first paying job you have ever had?

859. Have you ever been a volunteer?

860. If your work required you to move overseas for two years with the promise of a significant pay raise and promotion upon your return to your homeland, would you be willing to go?

861. What are your most important professional goals?

862. During the next five years, where do you see yourself professionally?

863. In the next ten years, where do you see yourself professionally?

864. During the next 20 years, what would you like to see in your professional life?

865. How would you define a workaholic? Are you one?

866. If you could own your own business, what would it be?

867. If you could start your whole professional life over again, but you had to choose another profession, what would it be and why?

868. What are the best and worst decisions you have made regarding your professional life?

869. Who is most proud of your professional success?

870. Before your life ends, what do you hope to achieve professionally?

871. How closely linked is your understanding of your life purpose to your profession? Explain.

872. Who is your professional role model, the person who has most closely achieved what you want to achieve?

873. Finish this statement. "I'll know I have succeeded when_____."

874. At what age would you like to retire? Is that realistic?

875. How well have you planned for retirement?

876. How and where would you like to spend your retired years?

877. Are you willing to lie for your employer?

878. What impact do you think gender has on a person's advancement in the workforce? Explain.

879. Describe a feeling you frequently have at work that is similar to a feeling you frequently had as a child.

880. Have you ever left one job for another that

paid less or seemed like a step down in order to be happy or prioritize your personal life?

881. What keeps you going to work besides a paycheck?

882. Why did you leave your last job?

883. Have you ever been fired? Why?

884. Would you rather have a boss or be the boss?

885. What irritates you about your co-workers?

886. What has been your greatest professional accomplishment?

887. What has been your biggest professional disappointment?

888. Do you work well under pressure?

MONEY

889. Are you comfortable discussing your finances with significant others? If not, explain.

890. If you could have money OR looks, which would you choose?

891. Did you receive an allowance as a child? What did you do with it?

892. At what age did you begin saving money? What was your reason for saving?

893. What were you financially responsible for as a child, adolescent, and teen, if anything?

894. Do you know where your money is spent? How would you describe (in percents) in categorical terms where your money goes? (For example, 50% living expenses, 20% savings, etc.).

895. How often do you have to pay overdraft fees on your checking account?

896. How much money would you like to be making per year five years from now?

897. If you could have the house of your dreams, but it would require you to forgo all entertainment, dining out experiences,

the new car you want, and new clothes and shoes for an entire year, would you buy the house?

898. Would you rather have a $50,000 wedding ceremony or make a down payment on a new home?

899. Have you ever stolen? Were you caught?

900. Are you more likely to research for weeks before purchasing a car or buy a vehicle on the spur of the moment?

901. If you were shopping for groceries and you had the option to save money by purchasing a generic brand of food, would you?

902. Do you hope to be financially wealthy some day? What is your definition of financial wealth?

903. Do you gamble? Describe.

904. In your opinion, what is the difference between someone who is financially secure and not financially secure?

905. Would you describe the socio-economic status of your family-of-origin as lower class, middle class, or upper class? Has that status changed from birth until now?

906. If you couldn't do both, would you rather do what you love and not make a lot of money or make a lot of money while not doing what you love?

907. If you had to choose, would you rather have a nice car, a nice house, or a nice wardrobe? Explain.

908. Describe your history with and feelings about credit card debt.

909. If you won a net sum of $2 million in the lottery, what would you do with the money?

910. Would you feel comfortable signing over your paycheck to your partner and having him manage your income entirely?

911. If you had to choose, would you rather bring home the bacon or fry it up in a pan? In other words, would you rather work or tend to the house?

912. Is money the root of all evil? Explain.

913. How would you feel and respond if you learned that your partner is a very poor financial manager?

914. If your partner has significantly more debt and a significantly lower income than you, would you be willing to combine finances after committing to him or her for life?

915. Can money buy you love?

916. Would you rate your credit score as poor, average, good, or excellent? Explain why.

917. Suppose your partner has an opportunity to pursue her lifetime dream to be a writer. It's

a long shot, and she needs 3 months to write without interruption. Would you support her both emotionally and financially to help her?

918. How important is saving money to you? What percentage of your income do you think needs to be designated to savings?

919. Imagine you have $50 that you could spend as you please today. What would you like to do with it?

920. Is it important to you to combine finances if you are in a committed relationship? Explain.

921. If you do not have enough money to pay all of your bills for the month, how are you likely to address this dilemma?

922. What percent of the total bill do you usually tip at a restaurant? How does bad service affect your tipping amount? Describe your tipping habits in general with hair stylists, massage therapists, cab drivers, and the like.

923. How would most people describe you when it comes to money? Do they categorize you as "tight," "loose," or "in between?"

924. If your partner was not comfortable discussing finances and wished to keep all assets separate and private, how would you feel? Does the length of time you are together or the level of commitment to one another change how you would feel about this?

925. How important is it to you that your financial contributions to your relationship are equal to, or greater than, your partner's? Explain.

926. Do you consider yourself competitive (with friends, partners, family, etc.) when it comes to the amount of income you make compared to them?

927. What are your views on philanthropic contributions such as donating to causes, churches, organizations, and other charity giving? What is your comfort level with financial contributions for important causes and purposes? At what set amount or percent of your salary are you comfortable donating to various causes?

928. Under what circumstances, if any, do you believe it is okay to file for bankruptcy? Have you ever filed for bankruptcy?

929. Describe the living arrangement you would like to have within the next five years. Is it a house, a condo, a cabin, or something else? Include the expense of the property, size, location, and other details as relevant.

930. What is the worst financial decision you've ever made? What's the best?

931. How has money had a positive influence on your life? How has it had a negative influence?

932. If you couldn't afford to buy your partner a

gift, how would you convey your love and appreciation for him or her?

933. What is the hardest thing for you to spend money on? What type of purchases do you get the most satisfaction out of making?

934. What is the first memorable thing you bought with your own money?

935. If you found $100 bill on the floor at the grocery store, what would you do with it?

FREE TIME, ENTERTAINMENT AND VACATIONS

936. If you could extend each day by 5 hours, what would you do during that time?

937. During your average week, how many hours do you spend watching television shows and movies at home?

938. What is your favorite thing to do on Sundays? Is it more important to you to spend your free time being productive or having fun?

939. If you were limited to (or in some cases, had to watch) one TV show a week, what would you watch?

940. Would you rather go to a nearby attraction for a week in order to stretch your vacation budget as far as it can go, or would you rather go to a distant location like a Caribbean island and have less money to spend while there?

941. How do you typically spend your weekends? Is this the way you want to spend them? If not, then why? How would you rather spend your weekend?

942. If you had to do without television, music, or books, which one would you let go?

943. What activities bring you the greatest joy?

944. If you could spend the afternoon taking a nap, doing a project around the house, taking a Sunday Drive, or going to a movie, which would you prefer and why?

945. What does your ideal vacation look like? You can consider the length, location, activities, food, people present, cost, transportation, and more.

946. If you were given the option to vacation in a tent, an RV, or a luxury resort, which would you prefer?

947. Can you swim? Who taught you and when?

948. Do you enjoy reading for pleasure? If so, what kind of books? Do you read the paper, magazines, journals, or other publications? Describe.

949. Order the following activities from the most desirable to the least: sharing a nice meal with friends, viewing a musical or play, attending a sporting event, going to a movie, or taking a long, scenic walk with your partner.

950. What do you consider a vacation? Traveling somewhere, taking time off, spending free time at home?

951. What was your best vacation as a child?

952. How many vacations per year do you consider realistically ideal?

953. Would you rather your vacations be planned and mapped out in advance, or do you prefer more spontaneity and adventure?

954. Would you rather spend a week on a beach, at a golf resort, or in another country sight-seeing?

955. Would you enjoy a week of vacation spent at home? How would you spend your "stay-cation?"

956. If your partner wanted you to go to a garage sale with him at 7am on a Saturday morning, would you go? If not, why?

THIS OR THAT

957. Would you rather initiate sex or have your partner initiate?

958. Would you rather shower or take a bath?

959. Would you rather have a pedicure or a massage?

960. Would you rather always lose or never play?

961. Would you rather be 10 inches taller or 10 inches shorter?

962. Would you rather be a president or a zookeeper?

963. Would you rather drive a speed boat or fly a plane?

964. Would you rather be rich and unattractive or poor and good looking?

965. Would you rather be stranded on an island alone or with someone you despise?

966. Would you rather find your soul mate or win a 10 million dollar lottery?

967. Would you rather seek revenge or peace?

968. Would you rather give bad advice or take bad advice?

969. Would you rather give up the internet or your pet?

970. Would you rather have three nipples or an extra finger?

971. Would you rather have the ability to fly or be invisible?

972. Would you rather have an amazing singing voice or be able to play an instrument flawlessly?

973. Would you rather know everything or have everything?

974. Would you rather kiss a stranger or hug someone you don't like?

975. Would you rather know or not know if you had a terminal illness?

976. Would you rather love someone who doesn't love you back or not love at all?

977. Would you rather work a menial job or make the same amount of money collecting unemployment?

978. Would you rather have a disorder that induces excessive, non-stop, but odorless sweating or a disorder that caused you to always smell like fish?

979. Would you rather go without your phone or your email?

980. Would you rather break a leg skydiving or by tripping down the stairs at work?

981. Would you rather see a pornographic movie with your parents or have a heavy make out session with your partner in a very busy, public park?

982. If you won the lottery, would you rather give 50% of your proceeds to charity or double your income by investing in the tobacco industry?

983. Would you rather have ten children or fifty indoor cats?

984. Would you rather have an unremoveable mole on the tip of your nose or a skin disease on both of your arms?

985. Would you rather fail or never try?

986. Would you rather be a donkey or an elephant?

987. Would you rather drive an unreliable, brand new BMW or a reliable 1970's VW Beetle?

988. Would you rather live to 105 and spend the last ten in a wheel chair or live to be 85 and be entirely healthy and independent?

989. Would you rather hold a burning match in your hand for 30 seconds or be submerged in a tub of icewater for 10 minutes?

990. Would you rather spend a year in jail or five years on house arrest?

991. Would you rather be 50 pounds overweight and healthy or skinny and chronically unhealthy?

992. Would you rather author a bestselling book or direct an award winning documentary?

993. Would you rather have one person in your life who would do anything for you or 50 people that you can always have a lot of fun with?

994. Would you rather be a cowboy or a pirate?

995. Would you rather go bowling or play darts?

996. Would you rather ride the world's longest roller coaster or swim far out in the open ocean?

997. Would you rather fart in front of a new date or get sick and throw up at dinner?

998. Would you rather walk on a cloud or walk on water?

999. Would you rather be seen picking your nose in public or be seen in an adult bookstore?

1000. Would you rather hug 10 random strangers or say "I love you" to three aquaintances?

MICHELE O'MARA, PHD

Michele O'Mara holds a PhD in Sexology from the American Academy of Clinical Sexologists and a Masters of Social Work from Indiana University-Purdue University (IUPUI). As a Licensed Clinical Social Worker (LCSW) and a Certified Imago Therapist, Michele provides Imago relationship counseling and sex therapy to couples. In addition to being an author, she has also created a personal growth series of classes called *Designing My Life*, and she regularly provides relationship workshops for couples. Thanks to the internet, she also offers relationship and life coaching to folks all across the nation via Skype.

WANT RELATIONSHIP COACHING?

Michele O'Mara is a skilled, sensitive, and well-educated therapist specializing in couples counseling and sex therapy. If you need relationship help, Michele O'Mara, PhD is available for in-office and internet based relationship coaching. Her relationship coaching services can reach anywhere there is a viable internet connection.

CONTACT INFO

Michele O'Mara, PhD
E-mail: michele@micheleomara.com